DASH Diet Slow Cooker Cookbook

*Quick & Easy to Prepare Recipes
For Your Slow Cooker!*

Disclaimer

All rights reserved. No part of this Book may be reproduced, stored in a retrieval system, or transmitted, in any form, or by any means, including mechanical or electronic, without the prior written permission of the author, nor be otherwise circulated in any form.

While the author has made every effort to ensure that the ideas, guidelines and information presented in this Book are safe, they should be used at the reader's discretion. The author cannot be held responsible for any personal or commercial damage arising from the application or misinterpretation of information presented herein.

Table of Contents

Disclaimer

Introduction

Chapter 1: DASH Diet and the Slow Cooker

    The DASH Diet Overview 9

    The Slow Cooker 11

Chapter 2: Slow-Cooked Soups

    Hearty Chicken Noodle Soup 13

    Light Chicken Tortilla Soup 16

    Minestrone Soup Mexican-Style 18

    Ground Beef Green Pepper Soup 19

    Split Pea, Vegetable and Ham Soup 20

    Vegetable Mushroom Barley Soup 21

    Chili Soup 24

    Wild Rice Soup 26

    Potato Cheesy Soup 28

Zucchini Soup..30

Chapter 3: Poultry Dishes on a Slow Cooker

Chicken and Rice 32

Chicken Noodle with Poppy Seed 34

Cheesy Mushroom Chicken..........................36

Chicken and Mexican-Style Salsa 38

Pulled BBQ Chicken 40

Chicken Stroganoff..41

Paprika Chicken...42

Turkey with Green Beans and Potatoes......44

Turkey Dinner..45

Barbecued Turkey..47

Turkey Sandwich...48

Ground Turkey with Cheesy Scalloped Potatoes 50

Chapter 4: Pork Cooked Slowly

Tender Pork Roast...52

Savory Herbs Pork Chop 54

Pineapple Pork 56

Creamy Mustard Pork 57

Jalapeño and Pecan Pork Chops 59

Chapter 5: Beef Slow Cooker Recipes

Stewed beef 61

Pulled Beef with Barbecue Sauce 64

Hearty Italian-Style Beef 66

Flank Steak Broil 68

Chili con Carne with Paprika 70

Meatballs with Lemon Sauce 72

Chapter 6: Slow-Cooked Vegetable Dishes

Collard Greens 75

Vegetable Stew 77

Lentil and Mixed Vegetable Stew 78

Chickpea and Cauliflower Stew 80

Vegetable and Tofu Curry 82

Hearty Vegetarian Chili 84

Butternut Squash and Apple Dish 86

Light Eggplant Parmesan 87

Vegan Jambalaya 89

Bean, Artichoke and Greens Ragout 92

Chapter 7: Slow Cooker Pasta Recipes

Slow Cooker Lasagna 97

Angel Hair Pasta Chicken 101

Spaghetti with Meatballs 103

Creamy Enchilada Orzo 105

Asparagus and Spinach Tortellini 107

Conclusion

Introduction

I want to thank you and congratulate you for purchasing the book, *"DASH Diet Slow Cooker Cookbook – Quick & Easy to Prepare Recipes for Your Slow Cooker!"*

This book contains proven steps and strategies on how to prepare simple and healthy recipes using the slow cooker that adhere to the philosophy of the DASH diet. DASH stands for Dietary Approaches to Stop Hypertension.

The DASH diet is gaining popularity and credibility as an excellent eating program for people who want to live a healthy lifestyle and lose weight. The slow cooker is an amazing cooking appliance that almost all homes have. This wonderfully versatile kitchen gadget allows families to eat tasty food with economical ingredients. It also offers a healthier cooking method. Utilizing the slow cooker in preparing DASH diet recipes is a great combination of healthy and delicious recipes that are not difficult to prepare.

In this book, the reader will discover many different DASH diet recipes using the slow cooker. It starts off with a short overview of the DASH diet and an introduction to the short cooker. The recipes presented here are separated according to different major ingredients and food types. They are divided into soups, chicken and turkey main dishes, pork main dishes, beef main dishes, vegetables and pasta. All these types of food can be prepared in a slow cooker. All the recipes were especially chosen to cater to different palates and tastes. They are all healthy, delicious and have easily-available and affordable ingredients.

Thanks again for purchasing this book. I hope you enjoy it!

Chapter 1: DASH Diet and the Slow Cooker

The DASH Diet Overview

The DASH Diet is an eating plan that is an acronym for Dietary Approaches to Stop Hypertension. It is an approach that uses foods such as low-fat dairy, whole grains, lean meats, legumes, vegetables and fruits. The ingredients recommended for this diet program are high in fiber, low in cholesterol, saturated fat and sodium, and rich in minerals such as potassium, magnesium and calcium.

The goal of the program is to make sure that individuals are making healthy food choices. It's gaining a considerable number of followers because it is flexible enough to cater to diverse lifestyles and preferences of people. Studies show that the DASH program not only helps people lose weight, but also reduces the risk of life-threatening illnesses such as heart disease, cancer, hypertension, stroke and diabetes. This is the reason that the DASH diet program has been ranked as the #1 diet in America, as identified by the US NEWS and World Report, for the past consecutive years. It is also a diet that is recommended by various medical associations in America.

It was not originally developed as a weight-loss program, but was a way to address the dietary needs of people with hypertension. Its main purpose is lowering the blood pressure of hypertensive people, and one of the effects of eating the right kinds of food just happen to be losing unwanted pounds. The DASH diet not only lowers blood pressure but retains it once it is lowered.

The Slow Cooker

Since the DASH diet advocates low-fat or fat-free ingredients, many DASH diet recipes are baked, broiled, grilled or roasted instead of fried. Ingredients such as beans and legumes, whole-wheat grains and protein substitutes are recommended in this type of diet. Lean cuts of meat and fat-free or reduced-fat dairy products are always used because they have less saturated fat.

The slow cooker lends itself well to the types of ingredients advocated by the DASH diet. That is the reason why there are many DASH diet recipes that use the slow cooker. Preparing food in a slow cooker does not require oil as long as there is enough moisture within it. This low-fat cooking method is ideal for those who are watching their cholesterol levels. All types of dishes that are prepared in a slow cooker are healthier and since the flavors have incorporated for a longer amount of time, they are also more flavorful.

Here are other benefits of preparing dishes using a slow cooker:

1. Slow cookers are economical to use. Slow cookers are perfect for cooking inexpensive cuts of meat like chicken thighs and pork shoulder. Less meat and more vegetables can also be used in a dish if there are budgetary restrictions. The slow-cooking method extracts more flavors from the meat and incorporates through the vegetables.

2. Slow cookers save time. Most dishes prepared in the slow cooker require all ingredients to be thrown in and combined together. Then you just leave it alone for a few hours and let the flavors incorporate. You can do your work or chores and the slow cooker will just get the job done. This is ideal for busy individuals.

The next few chapters will present delicious and easy recipes that could be prepared in a slow cooker. They are divided per type of course or main ingredient used.

Chapter 2: Slow-Cooked Soups

Hearty Chicken Noodle Soup

Serves 7

Ingredients:

4 cups low sodium chicken broth

2 boneless and skinless whole chicken breasts

4 ounces broken whole wheat spaghetti

1 sliced carrot

1 chopped celery stalk

1 peeled onion

3 cubed potatoes

3 whole garlic cloves

3 bay leaves

½ cup chopped dill

5 whole black peppercorns

7 cups boiled water

Salt and freshly ground black pepper

Procedure:

- a) Put chicken broth, water, chicken, carrot, onion, garlic, celery, whole black peppercorns and bay leaves in a slow cooker.

- b) Cook on low for 6 hours. Another option is to cook on high for 4 hours.

- c) Open the slow cooker after the designated number of hours and discard the peppercorns, whole onion, and bay leaves.

- d) Remove the chicken breasts and shred. Return the shredded chicken to the slow cooker. Add the potatoes and pasta.

- e) Cover and cook for 45 minutes.

- f) When ready to serve, season with salt and pepper and garnish with dill.

Light Chicken Tortilla Soup

Serves 8

Ingredients:

3 boneless and skinless chicken breasts

1 can 99% fat-free chicken broth

1 chopped onion

3 garlic cloves

1 can diced tomatoes

1 can enchilada sauce

1 package frozen corn

1 can chopped green chili peppers

1 tablespoon cumin

1 tablespoon chili powder

1 tablespoon chopped cilantro

1 bay leaf

2 cups water

Salt and black pepper

Procedure:

a) Mix all the ingredients in a slow cooker.

b) Cook on low for 6 hours. Another option is to cook on high for 4 hours.

c) Remove the chicken breasts and shred. Return the shredded chicken to the slow cooker.

d) Season with salt and pepper. Stir and serve.

Minestrone Soup Mexican-Style

Serves 12

Ingredients:

2 cans low-sodium vegetable broth

1 can chick peas

1 package frozen green beans

2 cups diced red potato

2 cans black beans

1 cup salsa

1 can sweet corn

2 cans stewed tomatoes

Procedure:
- a) Combine all ingredients in a slow cooker.
- b) Cook for 5 ½ hours on high setting.

Ground Beef Green Pepper Soup

Serves 6

Ingredients:

1 pound extra lean ground beef

1 chopped onion

1 cup cooked white rice

2 cups chopped green peppers

2 cups diced tomatoes

3 cups water

1 tablespoon beef bouillon

Salt and pepper

Procedure:

    a) Put all ingredients in a slow cooker.

    b) Cook in the slow cooker for 6 to 8 hours.

Split Pea, Vegetable and Ham Soup

Serves 8

Ingredients:

1 cup sliced celery

1 cup sliced carrots

1 cup sliced onion

2 cups of diced cooked ham

1 pound bag of dried split peas

6-8 cups water

Procedure:

a. Place all the ingredients in the slow cooker.

b. Cook in the slow cooker for 4 hours.

Vegetable Mushroom Barley Soup

Serves 4

Ingredients:

1 can rinsed and drained reduced-sodium kidney beans

1 can low-salt diced tomatoes

1 can low-salt chicken broth

3 cups fat-free milk

1 cup sliced mushrooms

1 stalked sliced celery

1 cup chopped onion

3 minced garlic cloves

1 sliced carrot

¼ cup cornstarch

½ cup frozen whole kernel corn

½ cup dry pearl barley

2 teaspoons dried oregano

¼ cup chopped parsley

Pepper

Procedure:

a. In a slow cooker, combine the beans, barley, corn, mushrooms, onion, tomatoes, garlic, carrot, celery, pepper and oregano. Stir in the broth.

b. Cook on low heat for 9 hours or on high heat for 5 hours.

c. 30 minutes before the end of cooking time, add cornstarch and milk into the slow cooker. Blend well.

d. The soup is ready when it has thickened. Sprinkle with fresh parsley and serve.

Chili Soup

Makes 8

Ingredients:

1 ½ pounds cubed boneless beef round steak

1 cup chopped onions

29 ounces diced peeled tomatoes

31 ounces drained dark red kidney beans

1 cup chopped carrots

15 ½ ounces tomato sauce

1 cup chopped bell pepper

½ teaspoon cayenne pepper

¼ teaspoon garlic powder

1 tablespoon oil

1 ½ cups water

Salt and pepper

Procedure:

    a. Brown the beef in a skillet.

b. Put the vegetables, spices and beef into a slow cooker.

c. Cook for 4 to 5 hours on low.

Wild Rice Soup

Ingredients:

1 pound sliced boneless and skinless chicken breasts

½ cup shredded carrot

½ cup chopped celery

½ cup flour

1 cup fat-free sour cream

½ cup chopped onion

8 ounces spinach leaves

3 cans fat-free chicken broth

½ cup wild rice

Procedure:

a. Mix all the ingredients except the sour cream, spinach and flour in a slow cooker.

b. Cook the slow cooker on low for 10-12 hours.

c. Add in the sour cream and flour. Increase the heat of the slow cooker to high and cook for a few minutes.

d. Add in the spinach and slowly stir until soup has thickened.

Potato Cheesy Soup

Serves 8

Ingredients:

4 cubed potatoes

2 stalks of chopped celery

1 shredded carrot

1 chopped onion

2 tablespoons chopped parsley

1 teaspoon paprika

2 tablespoons flour

2 cups fat-free shredded cheddar

1 cup nonfat milk

4 cups water

4 teaspoons chicken bouillon

Procedure:

a. Mix all ingredients in the slow cooker except for the cheese, flour and milk.

b. Cook for 8 hours in the slow cooker.

c. Mix the flour and milk in a mixing bowl, then add to the pot.

d. Stir the mixture well. Crank up the slow cooker on high. Cook for 20 more minutes.

e. Add the shredded cheese and serve.

Zucchini Soup

Ingredients:

1 ½ pounds Italian sausage

2 cups sliced celery

2 pounds sliced zucchini

2 cans diced tomatoes

1 cup chopped onion

2 sliced green bell peppers

1 teaspoon dried oregano

1 teaspoon Italian seasoning

1 teaspoon dried basil

¼ teaspoon garlic powder

1 teaspoon white sugar

6 tablespoons grated parmesan cheese

Salt

Procedure:

a) Cook sausage on a hot skillet for about 5 to 7 minutes. Combine the sliced celery into the sausage and cook for about 10 minutes or until the celery is tender.

b) Mix in the tomatoes, onion, salt, oregano, sugar, Italian seasoning, zucchini, bell peppers, basil, garlic powder and the sausage-celery mixture in a slow cooker.

c) Cook the slow cooker on low for 4 to 6 hours. Garnish with parmesan cheese.

Chapter 3: Poultry Dishes on a Slow Cooker

Chicken and Rice

Serves 6

Ingredients:

12 ounces boneless and skinless chicken

3 cans chicken broth

½ chopped onion

1 garlic clove

1 cup uncooked rice

1 can cream of mushroom soup

2 carrots

2 leeks

1 teaspoon thyme

½ teaspoon rosemary

Procedure:

a. Put the carrots, rice, leeks, garlic and onion in a slow cooker.

b. Mix in the thyme, rosemary and chicken. Season to taste.

c. Pour the chicken broth and mushroom soup over the mixture.

d. Cook on low heat for about 8 hours. Another option is to cook on high for 4 hours.

Chicken Noodle with Poppy Seed

Serves 4

Ingredients:

2 boneless and skinless chicken breasts

2 cups peas

4 cups whole wheat pasta

2 teaspoons poppy seeds

4 tablespoons fat-free butter or margarine

Salt and pepper

Procedure:

a. Bake the chicken until fully cooked through.

b. Boil the pasta until it is al dente.

c. Mix the baked chicken and the cooked pasta in the slow cooker.

d. Add in the rest of the ingredients.

e. Cook in the slow cooker for about 30 minutes or until the peas are warm and tender.

Cheesy Mushroom Chicken

Serves 6

Ingredients:

1 pound boneless and skinless chicken breast

1 box whole wheat penne pasta

1 can cheddar cheese soup (light version)

1 can cream of mushroom soup (light version)

1 cup Kraft 2% Mexican four-cheese blend

½ cup fat-free milk

Procedure:

a. Put the chicken breast in the slow cooker.

b. In a mixing bowl, mix the cheddar cheese soup and cream of mushroom soup with milk. Pour over the chicken on the slow cooker.

c. Cook on high for about 4 to 6 hours. Another option is to cook on low for about 8 to 10 hours.

d. Take out the chicken and shred.

e. Boil the pasta according to package directions.

f. Combine the pasta and shredded chicken and put them back with the soup mixture. Mix well.

g. Add the four-cheese blend and serve.

Chicken and Mexican-Style Salsa

Serves 6

Ingredients:

2 pounds boneless chicken breast

1 can of corn

2 cups of salsa

1 can diced tomatoes with green chili

1 chopped onion

Red pepper

Chili powder

Garlic powder

Onion powder

Ground oregano

Cumin

Procedure:

    a. Place the chicken in the slow cooker.

    b. Add spices with the chicken.

    c. Add onion, corn, tomatoes, salsa and green chili over chicken.

    d. Cook on low heat for 8 hours.

Pulled BBQ Chicken

Serves 4

Ingredients:

1 pound chicken breast

1 chopped onion

3 tablespoons brown sugar

½ cup low carbohydrate ketchup

1 can diet Pepsi

Procedure:

   a. Mix all ingredients in a slow cooker.
   b. Cook for about 6 hours.
   c. Remove the chicken after 6 hours and shred.
   d. Return the shredded chicken to the slow cooker. Cook for 1 more hour.
   e. Serve the chicken on buns or rolls.

Chicken Stroganoff

Serves 6

Ingredients:

1 pound boneless and skinless chicken breasts

16 ounces fat-free sour cream

1 can fat-free cream of mushroom soup

1 envelope dry onion soup mix

Procedure:

a. Put frozen chicken at the bottom of the slow cooker.

b. Combine soup, onion, sour cream and soup mix. Pour the mixture over the chicken.

c. Cook on low for 7 hours.

Paprika Chicken

Serves 4

Ingredients:

1 pound boneless and skinless chicken breasts

½ cup dry white wine

4 ounces sliced mushrooms

1 teaspoon mustard seeds

1 teaspoon cumin seeds

4 minced garlic cloves

1 sliced onion

1 tablespoon paprika

2 teaspoons olive oil

Garnish: sprigs of parsley

        Sweet red pepper rings

Procedure:

a. Heat oil in a skillet. Brown the chicken for 3 to 5 minutes on both sides.

b. Place the chicken on a slow cooker. Sprinkle the cumin, paprika, garlic and mustard.

c. Add more oil to the skillet where the chicken was cooked. Sauté the mushrooms and onions for about 2 to 3 minutes.

d. Spoon the sauce over the chicken in the slow cooker.

e. Cook on low for about 7 to 9 hours or until the chicken is tender.

f. Garnish with parsley and red pepper before serving.

Turkey with Green Beans and Potatoes

Serves 4

Ingredients:

1 package turkey smoked sausage

4 potatoes

1 can of green beans

Procedure:

a. Place the beans, potatoes and sliced sausages in the slow cooker.

b. Fill the slow cooker with water until all the ingredients are cover. Mix gently.

c. Slow cook for as long as possible.

Turkey Dinner

Ingredients:

1 ½ pounds turkey thighs (dark meat, skinless)

6 quartered red potatoes

1 can cream of mushroom soup

¼ cup all-purpose flour

1/3 cup chicken broth

2 tablespoons onion soup mix

2 cups sliced carrots

Procedure:

a. Place carrots and potatoes in a slow cooker. Add the turkey thighs.

b. In a mixing bowl, mix the flour with the remaining ingredients.

c. Pour the mixed ingredients into the slow cooker with the turkey and vegetables.

d. Cook on high for 30 minutes.

e. After 30 minutes, reduce to low and cook for about 7 hours.

f. Remove the turkey and vegetables from the slow cooker and put on a platter. Pour the sauce over them.

Barbecued Turkey

Serves 4

Ingredients:

3 sliced potatoes

6 carrots, sliced into sticks

1 cup barbecue sauce

2 turkey thighs (skinless and halved)

½ cup hot water

Procedure:

    a. In a mixing bowl, combine water and barbecue sauce. Mix well.

    b. Place the potatoes, carrots and turkey thighs in a slow cooker. Pour the barbecue sauce mixture over it.

    c. Cook on the slow cooker for 9 hours on low setting.

d. After 9 hours, remove turkey and vegetables and put on a serving platter. Pour the sauce over it.

Turkey Sandwich

Makes 12 sandwiches

Ingredients:

12 sandwich buns

½ cup brown sugar

¼ cup mustard

2 tablespoons apple cider vinegar

2 tablespoons ketchup

2 tablespoons hot pepper sauce

4 skinless turkey thighs

2 teaspoons liquid smoke

1 teaspoon crushed red pepper flakes

Salt and pepper

Procedure:

a. Use a non-stick cooking spray on a slow cooker.

b. Put the turkey inside the slow cooker.

c. Combine all remaining ingredients in a mixing bowl except for the sandwich buns. Mix very well.

d. Cook on low setting for 10 hours.

e. After 10 hours, remove the turkey, discard the bones and shred.

f. Return the shredded turkey to the broth and mix well.

g. When the turkey is ready, top them on the bottom half of the turkey buns to make a sandwich.

Ground Turkey with Cheesy Scalloped Potatoes

Serves 6

Ingredients:

1 pound ground turkey breast

½ teaspoon ground thyme

1 seeded and chopped red bell pepper

1 sliced onion

2 tablespoons margarine

1 ½ cups skim milk

2 ½ cups of boiling water

Hungry Jack Cheesy Scalloped Potatoes

Pepper

Procedure:

a. Heat oil on a skillet. When the oil is hot, place the ground turkey and cooked until brown.

b. Add the thyme and pepper.

c. In a mixing bowl, stir in sauce mix from the scalloped potatoes, sliced potatoes and margarine. Add boiling water and milk. Mix them well.

d. Put the browned turkey, onion and bell pepper in the mixing bowl.

e. Place all the mixture in a slow cooker. Add the potatoes and cover them with sauce.

f. Cook on low setting for 7 hours.

Chapter 4: Pork Cooked Slowly

Tender Pork Roast

Serves 6

Ingredients:

1 envelope onion soup mix

1 can cream of chicken soup (light)

12 pound sirloin tip pork roast

1 teaspoon dried thyme

1 teaspoon dried rosemary

¼ teaspoon dried pepper flakes

2 cups water

Pepper

Procedure:

a. Mix the onion soup and chicken soup mix with water in the slow cooker.

b. Add the pork roast and cook on low setting for 10 hours.

c. This is best served with rice.

Savory Herbs Pork Chop

Serves 2

Ingredients:

2 loin pork chops, fat-trimmed

1 peeled and cut onion

1 can of low-fat cream of mushroom soup

8 small potatoes

¼ teaspoon garlic powder

¼ cup white wine

1 teaspoon ground thyme

1 tablespoon fresh sage

1 tablespoon fresh rosemary

½ tablespoon olive oil

Salt and pepper

Procedure:

a. Put oil into a slow cooker.

b. Place potatoes and onions in the slow cooker. Sprinkle the garlic powder, rosemary, thyme and sage. Season with salt and pepper.

c. Add the vegetables. Lay the trimmed pork chops on top of the vegetables.

d. In a separate bowl, mix together the mushroom soup and wine. Pour the mixture over the pork chops and vegetables.

e. Cook on the slow cooker for 6 hours.

Pineapple Pork

Serves 4

Ingredients:

1 boneless pork roast

1 can pineapple chunks, with juice

1 cup chopped dried cranberries

Salt and pepper

Procedure:

a. Season the pork roast and put in a slow cooker.

b. Add the pineapple chunks with the juice and the dried cranberries.

c. Cook in the slow cooker for 7 hours on low setting.

Creamy Mustard Pork

Serves 8

Ingredients:

2 ½ pound pork sirloin roasts, fat-trimmed and boneless

¾ cup white wine

2 chopped carrots

1 chopped onion

¼ cup half and half

1 finely chopped shallot

2 tablespoons all-purpose flour

3 tablespoons Dijon mustard

1 tablespoon vegetable oil

Salt and pepper

Procedure:

a. Heat oil on a skillet. When the oil is hot, cook pork for 10 minutes.

b. Put the pork in a slow cooker. Add the remaining ingredients except for the half and half and the mustard. Pour the mixture over the pork.

c. Cook on a slow cooker for 9 hour or until pork is tender.

d. Remove the pork from the cooker and keep warm.

e. Add the half and half into the juices left in the slow cooker. Mix in the mustard into the juices.

f. Cook on the slow cooker for 15 minutes. Pour the sauce with the pork and serve.

Jalapeño and Pecan Pork Chops

Serves 6

Ingredients:

6 sliced loin pork chops (boneless, fat-trimmed)

¾ cup chopped celery

1 ¼ cups reduced-sodium chicken broth

1 lightly beaten egg

½ cup chopped pecans

¾ cup chopped onion

¼ cup jalapeño peppers

½ teaspoon dried rosemary

1 teaspoon rubbed sage

4 cups cornbread stuffing mix

Pepper

Procedure:

a. Heat oil on a skillet. When the skillet is hot, cook pork for 10 minutes or until browned. Set aside.

b. Using the same skillet, cook the onion, celery, jalapeño pepper, pecans, rosemary and sage. Season with black pepper. Cook for 5 minutes and set aside.

c. Mix cornbread stuffing, vegetable mixture and broth in a bowl. Mix well. Put the mixture in the slow cooker. Layer the pork on top of the stuffing. Cook on low setting for 5 hours.

Chapter 5: Beef Slow Cooker Recipes

Stewed beef

Serves 6

Ingredients:

1 ½ pounds sliced beef stew, fat-trimmed

1 can low-sodium beef broth

1/3 cup dry sherry

2 cups sliced fresh mushrooms

18 ounces carton light sour cream

2 cups cooked noodles

1 chopped onion

2 minced garlic

2 tablespoons cornstarch

½ teaspoon crushed oregano

¼ teaspoon crushed thyme

1 bay leaf

2 teaspoons vegetable oil

Salt

Optional: fresh parsley

Procedure:

a. Heat oil in a skillet. Cook the beef until brown. Drain off the fat.

b. Put the mushrooms, onion, garlic, oregano, thyme and bay leaf in a slow cooker. Season with salt and pepper.

c. Add the beef to the slow cooker. Pour the broth and sherry in the cooker.

d. Cook in the slow cooker on low heat for 10 hours. When done, remove and discard the bay leaf.

e. After 10 hours, turn to high heat.

f. Mix sour cream and cornstarch in a separate bowl. Whisk about 1 cup of the cooking liquid from into the sour cream and cornstarch mixture.

g. Add the sour cream mixture into the slow cooker. Cook for 30 more minutes.

h. Serve over noodles and sprinkle with parsley.

Pulled Beef with Barbecue Sauce

Makes 12 servings

Ingredients:

3 pounds boneless chuck roast

1 bottle of barbecue sauce

1 teaspoon onion powder

1 teaspoon garlic powder

Salt and pepper

Procedure:

a. Put the roast into the slow cooker.

b. Sprinkle it with garlic powder and onion powder.

c. Season with salt and pepper.

d. Pour the barbecue sauce.

e. Cook for 8 hours.

f. After 8 hours, remove the meat from the slow cooker. Shred the meat and return to the cooker. Cook for 1 hour. Serve hot.

Hearty Italian-Style Beef

Makes 6

Ingredients:

2 pounds boneless beef chuck pot roast, sliced

1 can low-salt beef broth

1 cup dry red wine

1 can tomato paste

2 tablespoons tapioca

8 ounces quartered new potatoes

2 sliced carrots

1 chopped onion

4 minced garlic cloves

2 cups fresh basil leaves

1 sliced fennel bulb

1 teaspoon crushed rosemary

Pepper

Procedure:

a. Put the potatoes, carrots, fennel and onions in a slow cooker. Add the meat and sprinkle with rosemary.

b. In a mixing bowl, mix the broth, tomato paste, wine, garlic, tapioca and garlic. Pour the mixture in a slow cooker.

c. Cook on low setting for 10 hours or on high setting for 5 hours.

d. Add the basil and serve.

Flank Steak Broil

Serves 8

Ingredients:

2 pounds flank steak

1 can light cream of mushroom soup

1 can light tomato soup

1 package dry onion soup mix

4 teaspoons of Worcestershire sauce

Procedure:

a. Put the meat at the bottom of the slow cooker.

b. Combine all the remaining ingredients in the mixing bowl.

c. Pour the mixture in the slow cooker on top of the meat.

d. Cook for 8 to 10 hours in the slow cooker.

e. After 10 hours, when the meat is done, remove it from the slow cooker and slice into small pieces.

f. Return the meat pieces back to the slow cooker. Cook for 30 more minutes.

Chili con Carne with Paprika

Serves 6

Ingredients (Spice Paste):

2 tablespoons dark chili powder

1 teaspoon hot paprika

2 teaspoons unsweetened cocoa powder

1 tablespoon cumin

1 chopped jalapeño

1 tablespoon cornmeal

3 tablespoons water

Ingredients (chili):

12 ounces cubed extra lean top sirloin

2 cups chicken stock

1 cup chopped onion

2 cups garlic cloves

1 can diced tomatoes, salt-free

2 cups diced carrots

1 can red kidney beans

1 can Great Northern beans

1 tablespoon vegetable oil

Procedure:

    a. Put all the spice paste ingredients in blender and mix until a paste is formed.

    b. Coat cooking spray in a skillet and heat. When the skillet is hot, stir in the beef. Cook until the meat is browned. Add the spice paste and cook for another minute until the paste has incorporated into the beef.

    c. Transfer the cooked meat and spices to the slow cooker.

    d. Add the remaining ingredients and cook in low setting for 6-8 hours.

Meatballs with Lemon Sauce

Serves 4

Ingredients:

1 pound lean ground beef

½ cup chopped green onions

¼ cup rolled oats

¼ cup frozen egg product

¼ teaspoon red pepper

3 teaspoons lemon peel

½ cup apricot fruit spread

2 tablespoons reduced-sodium soy sauce

2 tablespoon lemon juice

4 cups steamed pea pods

2 teaspoons cornstarch

¼ cup water

Nonstick cooking spray

Salt and freshly ground pepper

Optional: lemon wedges

Procedure:
a. Mix green onions, egg product, oats, lemon peel, crushed red pepper and salt in a bowl. Add the ground beef.

b. When well-combined, shape into meatballs.

c. Coat a skillet with cooking spray. When it is hot, brown the meatballs. Set aside.

d. In a separate mixing bowl, combine apricot fruit spread, water, soy sauce and lemon juice.

e. Combine the apricot mixture and meatballs and put them in the slow cooker.

f. Cook on low setting for 4 hours or on high setting for 2 hours.

g. Put the meatballs in a serving platter.

h. In a separate bowl, mix 1 tablespoon lemon juice, 1 tablespoon soy sauce, cornstarch and lemon peel. Add the mixture to the cooking liquid in the slow cooker. Add the sauce to the meatballs.

i. Sprinkle with black pepper and serve with wedges of lemon.

Chapter 6: Slow-Cooked Vegetable Dishes

Collard Greens

Serves 12

Ingredients:

6 ounces turkey necks (for flavoring)

2 pounds chopped collard greens

½ chopped onion

1 can fat-free chicken broth

3 tablespoons apple cider vinegar

2 teaspoons sugar

½ cup water

2 tablespoons olive oil

Salt

Procedure:
a. Put the turkey necks at the bottom of the slow cooker.
b. Stir in the collards and onions. Add the chicken broth and water.
c. Cook for 6 hours in high setting.
d. After 45 minutes, put the cider vinegar, sugar and olive oil in the slow cookers. Season to taste and mix well.

Vegetable Stew

Serves 6

Ingredients:

1 cup corn

1 cup hominy

1 cup chopped carrots

1 cup chopped celery

1 cup green beans

2 cups vegetable broth

1 small can tomato sauce

1 can black eyed peas

1 cup lima beans

2 tablespoons Worcestershire sauce

Salt and pepper

Procedure:

    a. Put all the ingredients in the slow cooker and cook for 8 hours in low setting.

Lentil and Mixed Vegetable Stew

Serves 8

Ingredients:

8 cups vegetable stock

1 bag dried lentils

2 cups chopped kale

1 can chopped tomatoes

1 chopped onion

2 chopped garlic cloves

2 chopped leeks

2 chopped carrots

3 chopped celery stalks

1 tablespoon fresh thyme

2 bay leaves

1 tablespoon olive oil

Kosher salt

Procedure:

a. Heat oil in a skillet. When hot enough, cook the onions for about 4 minutes or until translucent.

b. Add the garlic and cook for 1 minute more.

c. Put the onion and garlic mixture with the rest of the ingredients in the slow cooker and mix well.

d. Cook on high setting for 4 hours or on low setting for 8 hours. Check if the lentils are tender.

Chickpea and Cauliflower Stew

Serves 6

Ingredients:

2 diced celery stalks

1 can crushed tomatoes

2 cups vegetable broth

1 diced onion

2 minced garlic

3 sliced carrots

3 cups cooked chickpeas

1 sliced red pepper

½ teaspoon ground cinnamon

2 teaspoons ground cumin

1/8 teaspoon cayenne pepper

½ teaspoon ground ginger

1 teaspoon paprika

Salt and pepper

Procedure:

a. Put celery, onion and red pepper in a slow cooker. Add all the spices and stir for 1 minute.

b. Add all the vegetables and vegetable broth, making sure that everything is covered with water.

c. Cook in the slow cooker for 4 hours over high setting or 6 hours over low setting.

Vegetable and Tofu Curry

Serves 4

Ingredients:

16 ounces drained tofu

1 cup vegetable broth

1 chopped eggplant

1 chopped onion

¾ cups peas

1 ½ cups sliced bell pepper

¼ cup Thai green curry paste

1 can low-fat coconut milk

1 tablespoon coconut sugar

1 tablespoon minced ginger

½ teaspoon turmeric

Salt

Procedure:

a. Prepare the tofu by draining excess water with a paper or kitchen towel.

b. Place vegetable broth, coconut milk, green curry paste, turmeric, ginger, salt and coconut sugar to the slow cooker. Mix well.

c. Add the peas, bell pepper and eggplant. Cook the vegetables and broth mixture on high setting for 4 hours.

d. Slice the tofu. Heat a skillet with oil spray. When skillet is hot, cook the tofu until golden. Set aside.

e. When the curry mixture in the slow curry has 30 minutes left to cook, add the golden tofu. Cook for 30 more minutes.

Hearty Vegetarian Chili

Serves 8

Ingredients:

1 package drained and cubed tofu

2 cans crushed tomatoes

4 cans of black beans, drained

4 chopped onions

4 minced garlic cloves

2 chopped green bell peppers

2 chopped red bell peppers

6 tablespoons chili powder

2 teaspoons ground cumin

2 tablespoons dried oregano

2 tablespoons distilled white vinegar

1 tablespoon liquid hot pepper sauce

½ cup olive oil

Salt and freshly ground pepper

Procedure:

a. Heat olive oil in a skillet. When the skillet is hot, add the onions and cook until translucent.

b. Add the green and red bell peppers, tofu and garlic. Cook for about 10 minutes.

c. Put the black beans into the slow cooker. Add the cooked vegetables and tomatoes. Add cumin, oregano, chili powder, hot pepper sauce and vinegar. Season with salt and pepper. Stir well.

d. Cook on low setting for 8 hours.

Butternut Squash and Apple Dish

Serves 10

Ingredients:

1 pound peeled and cubed butternut squash

4 peeled, cored and chopped apples

½ diced white onion

¾ cup dried cranberries

1 tablespoon ground cinnamon

1 ½ teaspoons ground nutmeg

Procedure:

    a. Mix squash, cranberries, apples, cinnamon, onion and nutmeg in a slow cooker.

    b. Cook on high setting for 4 hours or until the squash is tender.

Light Eggplant Parmesan

Serves 8

Ingredients:

4 peeled and sliced eggplants

2 eggs

1/3 cup bread crumbs

3 tablespoons whole-wheat flour

1/3 cup water

½ cup grated low-sodium parmesan cheese

1 jar marinara sauce, low-sodium version

1 pack low-sodium sliced mozzarella cheese

1 cup olive oil

Salt

Procedure:

a. Layer the eggplant slices in a bowl. Season them with salt. Let them stand for 30 minutes to drain. Dry with kitchen or paper towels.

b. Combine eggs with water and whole-wheat flour. Stir well. Dip the eggplant slices in the batter.

c. Heat oil in a skillet. Fry the eggplant slices until golden brown.

d. Mix bread crumbs and parmesan cheese in a separate bowl.

e. Layer the eggplant slices on the slow cooker. Top with the crumb and cheese mixture, then with the marinara sauce and mozzarella cheese.

f. Layer three times and cook on low setting for 5 hours.

Vegan Jambalaya

Serves 6

Ingredients:

1 can diced tomatoes

1 cup vegetable broth

1 cup rice

½ chopped onion

2 minced garlic cloves

½ chopped green bell pepper

3 chopped celery stalks

8 ounces cubed seitan

8 ounces sliced smoked Vegan sausage

1 tablespoon miso paste

½ teaspoon dried thyme

½ teaspoon dried oregano

1 tablespoon chopped fresh parsley

1 ½ teaspoons Cajun seasoning

1 tablespoon olive oil

Procedure:

a. Put olive oil at the bottom of a slow cooker.

b. Add tomatoes with juice, vegan sausage, seitab, onion, celery, green bell pepper, garlic, miso paste, vegetable broth, thyme, oregano and Cajun seasoning. Mix well.

c. Cook on low setting for 4 hours. After 4 hours, add rice and cook on high setting until rice is cooked.

d. Garnish with parsley before serving.

Bean, Artichoke and Greens Ragout

Ingredients (ragout):

3 cups sliced leeks

1 cup sliced carrot

1 can diced tomatoes

1 cup chopped red bell peppers

1 ¾ cups vegetable broth

2 cups Swiss chard

1 package artichoke hearts

3 cups cooked cannellini beans

2 cups cubed red potato

2 ½ cups chopped fennel bulb

3 minced garlic cloves

1 teaspoon dried basil

¼ teaspoon dried oregano

1 tablespoon olive oil

¾ cup water

Salt and black pepper

Ingredients (relish):

6 sun-dried tomatoes

1 cup diced yellow bell pepper

3 cups shredded fennel bulb

¼ cup fresh parsley

1 tablespoon juice of lemon

1 cup boiling water

2 tablespoons olive oil

½ teaspoon sugar

Salt and black pepper

Procedure (ragout):

a. Heat oil in a skillet. Stir in the carrot, leek and garlic. Cook for 5 minutes or until the vegetables are tender.

b. Place the carrot and leek mixture in a slow cooker. Add beans and the rest of the ragout ingredients. Cook on high setting for 8 hours. Add the chard after 8 hours.

Procedure (relish):

a. Combine boiling water and sun-dried tomatoes in a bowl. Let it stand for 15 minutes until the tomatoes are soft. Drain the water and chop the tomatoes into small pieces.

b. Combine the chopped sun-dried tomatoes and the other relish ingredients.

Chapter 7: Slow Cooker Pasta Recipes

Slow Cooker Lasagna

Serves 8

Ingredients:

1 pound lean ground turkey

1 whisked egg

1 cup corn kernels

1 cup peeled and grated carrots

1 diced onion

2 cups Mexican cheese blend

2 jars mild chunky salsa

1 minced garlic clove

1 teaspoon ground cumin

½ teaspoon chili powder

¼ cup chopped cilantro

½ cup sour cream

12 corn tortillas

1 tablespoon olive oil

Salt

Procedure:

a. Heat 1 tablespoon of oil in a skillet. Cook the onions until translucent. Add the garlic and sauté for another minute.

b. Add the ground turkey meat, salt, cumin and chili powder and cook for 7 minutes. Set aside the turkey mixture.

c. In a mixing bowl, whisk the sour cream and egg. Add the cooked turkey mixture. Stir in the carrots, corn and cilantro. Mix well.

d. On the bottom of the slow cooker, layer one cup of salsa.

e. Layer 5 tortillas on top of the salsa. Cover the salsa completely.

f. Place the turkey mixture on the tortillas. Layer on top with 1 cup of salsa and ½ cup of cheese.

g. Add one more layer of tortillas, salsa, turkey mixture and cheese. Top with ½ cup of cheese.

h. Cook on low setting for 2 ½ hours.

Angel Hair Pasta Chicken

Serves 5

Ingredients:

1 ½ pound sliced boneless and skinless chicken thighs

½ pound uncooked angel hair pasta

4 ounces light Philadelphia cream cheese

1 can reduced-sodium cream of mushroom soup

¼ cup dry white wine

¼ cup Kraft Tuscan House Italian Dressing

2 tablespoons fresh parsley

Procedure:

a. Combine all the ingredients except for the pasta in a slow cooker. Cook on low setting for 4 hours.
b. Cook pasta based on package directions.

c. Serve the pasta topped with chicken mixture. Top with parsley.

Spaghetti with Meatballs

Serves 8

Ingredients:

1 pound spaghetti

1 ½ pounds ground beef

½ pound ground pork

1 can drained tomatoes

1 can tomato puree

1 beaten egg

2 teaspoons minced garlic

¼ cup dry bread crumbs

¼ cup grated low-fat parmesan cheese

3 tablespoons fresh parsley

1 teaspoon dried basil

¼ teaspoon crushed red pepper

2 tablespoons olive oil

Salt and pepper

Procedure:

a. In a mixing bowl, stir in beef, pork, cheese, bread crumbs, egg, garlic, parsley and olive oil. Season them with salt and pepper. Shape into meatballs.

b. In a slow cooker, put the tomato puree and canned tomatoes, red pepper and basil. Season with salt. Add the meatballs. Cook on low setting fro 6 hours.

c. Cook the spaghetti. Top the meatball sauce on top of the spaghetti.

Creamy Enchilada Orzo

Serves 6

Ingredients:

2 cups uncooked orzo pasta

1 can diced tomatoes

4 ounces cubed light cream cheese

1 cup canned black beans

1 cup kernels

½ cup vegetable broth

1 can mild enchilada sauce

2 tablespoons chopped cilantro leaves

1 can chopped green chilies, drained

Salt and pepper

Procedure:

a. In a slow cooker, enchilada sauce, tomatoes, vegetable broth, green chilies, black beans and corn. Season them with pepper and salt. Mix well. Top the mixture with cheese.

b. Cook on low setting for about 8 hours.

Asparagus and Spinach Tortellini

Saves 6

Ingredients:

2 cups spinach

2 diced tomatoes

1 cup sliced asparagus

1 dash shredded parmesan cheese

1 package garlic and white wine marinade

32 ounces vegetable broth

3 cups water

¾ cups white wine

20 ounces cheese tortellini

10 diced basil leaves

Procedure:
- a. Mix all the ingredients in a slow cooker except for the tortellini.

b. Cook on slow cooker in low setting for 8 hours or on high setting for 4 hours.

c. Add tortellini in the last hour.

d. Top cooked tortellini with a dash of shredded parmesan cheese.

Conclusion

Thank you again for purchasing this book!

I hope this book was able to help you to understand the principles of the DASH diet and how it can help you lead a healthy life. I hope that you are also able to see the advantage of using the slow cooker and how it is the perfect cooking gadget for people who are on the DASH diet. The healthy and delicious slow cooker recipes presented in the book are versatile and use a variety of ingredients that is flexible to any lifestyle or food preference. The simple procedures of preparing food using a slow cooker are also beneficial for busy people.

The next step is to choose the first recipe that suits your food preference and lifestyle and try it out. Happy cooking and eating!

Thank you and good luck!

Made in the USA
Lexington, KY
03 January 2017